Patrick Hawes

The Call

from *The Call*
for solo soprano and harp
(1997)

NOVELLO

The Call

from *The Call*

GEORGE HERBERT
(1593–1633)

PATRICK HAWES

length:_____ Such_ a Strength, as makes his Guest._____ Come,_

_ my Joy,_____ my Love, my Heart:_____ Such a Joy, as none can move:_____

Such a Love,_____ as none can part:_____ Such_ a Heart, as joys in

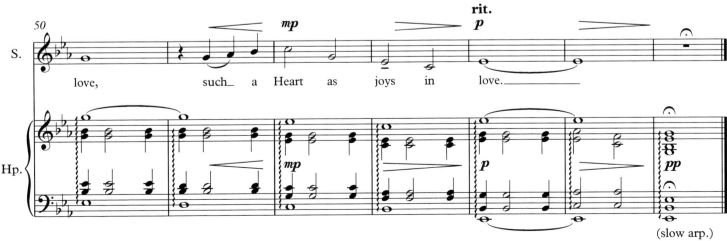

love, such a Heart as joys in love._____

(slow arp.)